OVERCOMING FEAR

BY

MARGARET FEINBERG

FOREWORD BY

LUCI SWINDOLL

NASHVILLE DALLAS MEXICO CITY RIO DE JANEIRO BEIJING

Published in Nashville, Tennessee by Thomas Nelson, Inc., P.O. Box 141000, Nashville, Tennessee 37214.

Thomas Nelson, Inc. titles may be purchased in bulk for educational, business, fundraising, or sales promotional use. For information, please email SpecialMarkets@ThomasNelson.com.

Published in association with the literary agency of Yates & Yates, Inc.

ISBN-10: 1-4185-2638-X
ISBN-13: 978-1-4185-2638-2

Printed in the United States of America.

HB 08.03.2021

✦ Contents ✦

✦ Foreword ✦

There are countless reasons for fear. They lie in the past, present, and future. Generally speaking, I'm not a person who's afraid very often, but when I am, the first thing that comes to my mind is to *pray*. It helps me to shift the weight of something too heavy for me onto the shoulders of our Almighty God.

I remember a few times in particular when I was afraid:

In the early 1970s, I moved from Texas (where I'd lived all my life) to California, and within months I began to question the wisdom of that move. Everything about it frightened me—my job, new friends, a different lifestyle—and I so wanted to run back home, even though that prospect frightened me even more. *What would people think if I came running back?* I felt stuck, and for two years I was virtually buried by fear of both the known and unknown that surrounded me. I prayed fervently about what to do. Lovingly, God showed me I needed to "let go" of the control I wanted over my life and to allow him to take the lead. Within weeks, I was actually offered another job that resulted in growth and opportunities I never dreamed possible. It also taught me that God knows so much more about what I need in my life than I do.

Then, in the early 1980s, my supervisor at Mobil Oil Corporation retired and I moved into his job. I was the first woman in a management position in that branch of the company. *Could I do the job? Was I qualified? Did I know enough?* All those fears plagued me and I was afraid to say yes, but more afraid to say no. I began asking the Lord what to do, and he led me to just the right people who prayed with me and knew how to encourage me to make the job work. That position was not only totally enjoyable for the three years I held it, but also opened the door for me to take early retirement to become an author and speaker, the work I love doing to this day.

And most recently, I had a questionable mammogram that necessitated a biopsy. Oh my! How scary is *that* unknown? Once again I took my burden to the Lord and was assured by his Word and promise that no matter what, he would never leave me nor forsake me in the outcome. He gave me peace.

This study guide addresses numerous fears and how we can face them through the power of Jesus Christ. It identifies the various sources of our fears, challenges us to claim God's promises, and offers counsel on how to turn our fears over to God. I wholeheartedly recommend it to you for your own study and encouragement.

I once read that fear is a darkroom where negatives are developed. Don't let yourself live in that room! Move into the light and allow the overcoming truth of God's Word to give you the faith you need to enjoy a life of freedom.

—Luci Swindoll

✦ INTRODUCTION ✦

THE SUM OF ALL FEAR

Did you know that fear can be *good* for you? No, really! A healthy amount of fear serves as a reminder to avoid danger. It can help us be more safety-conscience. The awareness that something bad could happen often causes us to do something good. Put on a seat belt. Wear a safety helmet. Don't play in the street. Stay away from the edge of the cliff.

A healthy dose of fear keeps us safe, but unhealthy fear is paralyzing. It prevents us from experiencing and living the life God intended. It limits our potential. Fear can hinder us from enjoying rich relationships, amazing experiences, and a meaningful life.

Fear can even stop us from fulfilling the call that God has on our lives. Left unchecked, fear can tie us to the past, push us toward sin, and prevent us from embracing our God-ordained future. That's one reason we find the same phrase echoing throughout the Bible: "Fear not!" Through his Son, Jesus, God has set us free from the unhealthy fears that bind us and hold us back.

Over the years, I have wrestled with countless fears—fear of failure, fear of rejection, fear of losing the things I hold dear. But God is continually asking me to let go of my fear, and to hold onto him. He is challenging me to exchange fear for faith.

Some fears may seem small or silly, but that doesn't make them seem any less real. One fear I've had since childhood that has never really gone away is the fear of being alone in the dark. Ever since I was a small girl, I have been a little jumpy when it comes to strange noises in the middle of the night. Even recently, when my husband went on a business trip, I found myself all alone tucked under several layers of bedding for extra protection.

Staring into the darkness, I heard a loud sound downstairs. Fear instantly gripped my heart. I lay perfectly still, breathing as quietly as possible. Then God's Spirit reminded me that I did not have to face the fear alone. I began to pray. I asked God for his protection. Within a few seconds, I began to sense his peace. Then, I began to feel courageous. I reached up and flipped on the light switch and went downstairs.

I recognized the culprit: a piece of Tupperware had fallen on the floor. Placing it carefully on the counter, I turned the light back off and tucked myself back into bed. I didn't need quite so many covers after all. And I enjoyed a sweet night's sleep.

As I had to face the frightening noise, all of us will eventually have to face our fears if we want to overcome them. The good news is that we do not have to do it alone. God promises to not only go with us but before us. There is no situation he cannot handle. There is no fear that cannot be overcome through his grace, strength, and protection.

Rest assured that God is bigger than any fear you may face.

Through this study, may God set you free from the sum of any and all fears—whether big or small—and may you learn to embrace the fullness of life that comes with being a child of God.

—Margaret Feinberg

CHAPTER 1

Outside My Comfort Zone

"For God did not give us a spirit of timidity, but a spirit of power, of love and of self-discipline."

2 Timothy 1:7

Almost everyone feels a little uneasy from time to time—especially when we are pushed outside our comfort zones. Such anxiety is often characterized by a fearful uncertainty or a sense of dread. You may feel anxiety about public speaking, taking tests, flying, confined spaces, or discovering a spider in your bed!

Those moments of anxiety can actually become phobias when they take root in our lives in the form of intense and irrational fears. For example, a person with apiphobia has a fear of bees. Now lots of people experience a sense of apprehension around bees—and for good reason, since no one wants to get stung! Some people are even radically allergic to bees and for medical reasons need to avoid them at all cost. But even mention bees to a person with apiphobia, and you can trigger a physical response as strong as if they were being stung. It's a good example of healthy apprehension becoming a paralyzing phobia.

From time to time one fear that keeps resurfacing in my own life is the fear of flying. Both my husband and I spend a lot of time traveling for work, and for whatever reason, every so often

I will find myself gripped by a paralyzing fear. On a recent flight, as we began our descent, I felt a sudden sharp fear that something was wrong with the aircraft. Though I hadn't heard any strange noises or felt any turbulence, I felt my chest tighten and breath quicken. I could barely move.

I began to pray, *Dear God, please help*.

I looked over at the passenger next to me, and he was completely relaxed, even peaceful. I compared his demeanor to my own and realized the fear I was experiencing was irrational. Simply by looking at someone who wasn't gripped by fear, I realized that I didn't need to be fearful either. I took a deep breath. Through the calming presence of a stranger, God answered my prayer.

Our loving Father does not want us to be controlled by anxiety, fear, or phobias. He wants us to be set free from all types of unhealthy fears no matter how large and looming or small and subtle.

The truth is that everyone wrestles with some type of fear—no matter how perfect or put together they may seem on the outside. Whatever fears you face, you are not alone. With God's help, you can overcome your fears and live by faith.

1. As we begin this study, what are some fears you remember from childhood that you now consider silly or have grown out of? What was the source of those fears? How did you get past them?

2. As you've grown older, what new fears have manifested themselves in your life? How are these fears different from the ones you faced as a child?

3. Take a moment to read **Psalm 91:5–10**. Reflecting on this passage, make a list of the types of fears mentioned. What would be the modern equivalent of these fears for you?

terror of night - fear of unknown
arrow that flies by day - Satan's deceptions.
pestilence that stalks in darkness - unexpected happenings
destruction that lays waste at noon - (sudden death)
1,000 at side 10,000 rt hand - wars, invasion of Ukraine
witness the divine repayment of the wicked
plague come near your tent - COVID ?

4. As you study Psalm 91:5–10, it's important to note that God never promises that fears and even real danger will not come. What does he promise instead? Why is it so important to put your faith in God?

You won't be afraid - danger won't come near -
You will be an observer because God is your
shelter.

Not only does fear limit your ability to place your faith in God, but if left unchecked, fear can also actually cause you to pull back from your relationship with God, choose to sin, and miss out on God's best for your life.

5. Read **Genesis 3:1–13**. Fear plays a significant role in the story of the fall of man. What does fear compel Adam to do in Genesis 3:10? How does fear shape Adam's response to God in Genesis 3:12? Can you think of any situations where you've been tempted to respond as Adam does?

Fear made Adam hide from God. Also contribute to blaming Eve. Fear undermines healthy relationships with ~~God~~ and others.

6. Read **Genesis 18:1–15**. In this passage, three visitors deliver an important prophetic message to Abraham and Sarah: Despite her age, within a year Sarah will have a child. Yet fear caused Sarah to sin. According to Genesis 18:15, what sin did Sarah commit? Can you think of a sin that fear has either tempted or caused you to commit?

Sarah denied that she had laughed – lied. Also unbelief

7. Read **Numbers 14:5–9**. Joshua and Caleb spied out the incredibly rich and abundant land into which God wanted to lead the Israelites. Reflecting on this passage, why was it so important that the people not fall prey to fear? Why is it so important that you don't fall prey to fear in your own life?

Fear would prevent the people from defeating the "giants" of the land and the people would forfeit God's best plan for their lives because of their fear

The truth is that there is no fear from which God cannot set you free!

The biblical accounts of Adam, Sarah, and the Israelites reveal just how much fear can affect your faith. Unhealthy fear causes you to hide from God, engage in sinful behavior, and can hold you back from all that God has for you.

8. Spend a few minutes in prayer, and ask God to reveal any fears that have a grip on you. Make a list below. Take a few minutes to pray about each one, asking God for forgiveness, freedom, and redemption.

First step in being free from fear, anxiety & worry is to ID fears that Satan tells us - lies - and change your thinking by taking every thought captive to Christ and renew mind by believing God's word.

✦Digging Deeper✦

Read Genesis 31:22–31. Jacob recognizes that he has lost favor with his father-in-law, Laban, and with God's leading, he packs up his family and children to head back to his homeland. What is Laban's complaint in Genesis 31:26–28? What does Jacob list as the motivating factor for his secret departure in Genesis 31:31? Can you think of any situations where your fear has affected or hurt a particular relationship in your life? What steps do you need to take to bring healing to that relationship?

✦Ponder and Pray✦

The opening Scripture for this lesson comes from 2 Timothy 1:7 and it reminds us, "For God has not given us a spirit of fear, but of power, and of love, and of a sound mind."

Think of a moment when God took away a "spirit of fear" in your life and replaced it with his spirit of "power, of love, and of sound mind." How did that experience affect your faith? Your relationships? Your attitude toward God?

✦ Notes & Prayer Requests ✦

Nancy Sharon - tumor
Dana
JP
Dick
Don
Maris
Mary Jane & Jim
Jim
Blaine
Linda - alcoholism
Zach - 26th
Pauline's foot
Ruthann's wrist
Joe Rassetti
Muriel
Basics - older people's safety
Mexican - American border
Linda - Steve's wife
our country

✦ Notes & Prayer Requests ✦

grandchildren & children
& brains

LETTING GO OF THE PAST

"DO NOT BE AFRAID; YOU WILL NOT SUFFER SHAME. DO NOT FEAR DISGRACE; YOU WILL NOT BE HUMILIATED. YOU WILL FORGET THE SHAME OF YOUR YOUTH AND REMEMBER NO MORE THE REPROACH OF YOUR WIDOWHOOD."

Isaiah 54:4

On a warm, sunny afternoon my mother and I were snorkeling off a small island in the Bahamas. As we floated alongside our dinghy in the outgoing tide, the shallow turquoise waters unveiled underwater gardens of colorful coral, brightly-colored fish, and layers of hidden beauty.

Suddenly, my mother grabbed my arm, removed the snorkel from her mouth, and said, "Get in the dinghy, now!" From the sternness in her voice, I knew something was seriously wrong. I didn't question. I didn't hesitate. I quickly lifted my body over the side of the small boat. She was seconds behind me.

"What was it?" I asked.

An eleven-foot hammerhead shark! My mother explained that she had been enjoying the colorful reef when she felt an unmistakable uneasiness. She looked behind her and saw the enormous shark cruising along less than a body's length behind us. It took her breath away, and she knew we needed to get out of the water—immediately.

At the time, I was only eight years old. Though I never actually saw the shark, the experience has never left me. It opened the doorway for an unhealthy fear in my life. It is a fear that didn't just last for the rest of our time in the Caribbean or even the rest of the summer. The truth is, the fear never really left. That one experience from my childhood has marked me with an irrational fear of sharks.

This fear surfaces every time I am in the ocean. And after all these years, the only way I know how to fight it is through prayer. At times I literally pray for God's protection as I swim and snorkel. I pray for his protection before I ever step foot in the water and thank him for it as I dry off.

Over the years, thanks to God's healing and grace in my life, my fear of sharks has lessened. Now, that doesn't mean I don't feel afraid sometimes, but I've learned to take that fear to God. In response, he reminds me that I am not alone, that the past is just that—the past, and that his protection is all-sufficient. Because of God, I can still spend an afternoon snorkeling in awe of his beautiful underwater creation.

Though you may have never encountered an eleven-foot hammerhead shark (I hope!), you have encountered things in your childhood, in your growing-up years, and elsewhere in your past that have been just as scary and sometimes more scarring. Such incidents can open up the doorway to a lifelong struggle with fear. But God in his love and grace wants you to move beyond the fear of the past so you can move into the hope of your future.

1. Take a moment to reflect on your past. Can you think of an instance like mine with the hammerhead shark when something happened, either to you or to someone you love, that filled your heart with fear? In what ways does that fear affect you today? How have you handled or responded to that fear in your life?

Proverbs 22:6 says, "Train a child in the way he should go, and when he is old he will not turn from it." The verse implies that the way a child is trained is crucial to the way he or she will live as an adult. That training should include blessings, wise discipline, and encouragement for the child to become all that he or she can be for God's glory. But unfortunately, not all training is beneficial for children. Sometimes parents inadvertently teach their children things that simply aren't from God—like fear! If a parent has an irrational fear, they can accidentally (or even intentionally) pass their unhealthy fear to their child.

2. Did you learn any unhealthy fears from one or both of your parents? How has that fear affected your life? Your relationships? Your ability to make wise decisions?

3. Reflecting on your own life, have you been tempted to train anyone else—a child, friend, or family member—in the way of an unhealthy fear? What steps do you need to take to stop spreading the anxiety and break the cycle of fear in your own life?

If left unchecked, a fear-filled encounter can become the foundation that you build your life on. One bad experience can shade and shape your future life decisions, yet God does not want your life to be built on anything but him.

4. Read **Isaiah 44:6–8**. What words does God use to describe himself? How do these words affect the way you think of God?

King of Israel & his Redeemer, Lord of Hosts, First & Last. No other God besides me. Don't be afraid, long ago proclaimed it, no other Rock

5. Why do you think God describes himself as a "Rock"? What comes to mind when you think of a rock? Why should you choose God, rather than an experience from your past, as your foundation?

Steady, good foundation - Carol & Paul

The Bible teaches that experiences from your past do not have to bind you in fear. Not only can you be set free from them, but you can use those experiences as reminders of God's power and protection. They can be used to help you face the challenges in your life *today*. Take a moment and reflect on this passage from the life of David found in **1 Samuel 17:32–37**.

6. How did God use David's encounter with the lion and bear to instill faith, rather than fear, into David's heart?

attributed victories against lion
& bear to God

7. As in the life of David, God often uses little experiences to prepare us for big encounters. What experiences from your own past does God want you to view as a source of faith rather than fear?

Moving from house
fall on ice

8. How can overcoming fear in your own life help others overcome their fears? What specific experience from your past does God want to use to help you encourage others?

The truth is that there is no experience from your past that cannot be overcome and redeemed!

✦DIGGING DEEPER✦

When faced with an irrational fear, Scripture can help remind us that our foundation is in God. Romans 12:2 challenges us, "Do not conform any longer to the pattern of this world, but be transformed by the renewing of your mind. Then you will be able to test and approve what God's will is—his good, pleasing and perfect will." God's Word is a powerful tool in renewing your mind and reminding you that he is your foundation.

Take a moment to reflect on the Bible passages mentioned so far in this study as well as any others you know. What Scripture can you commit to memory as a reminder that God is your Rock, the foundation of your life?

perfect peace - Is 26:3-4 Rock!
Isa 44:9-10

✦Ponder and Pray✦

The opening Scripture for this lesson comes from Isaiah 54:4, and it reminds us, "Do not be afraid; you will not suffer shame. Do not fear disgrace; you will not be humiliated. You will forget the shame of your youth and remember no more the reproach of your widowhood." Sometimes fears from our past are accompanied by feelings of shame, disgrace, and humiliation. Yet God wants to restore us and make us new. He wants us to "remember no more the reproach."

If you have asked for God's forgiveness, he is faithful to forgive! But sometimes the hardest person to forgive is yourself. Is there anything holding you back from forgiving yourself for something that happened in the past?

✦ Notes & Prayer Requests ✦

Chapter 3

Running Toward the Future

"When you pass through the waters, I will be with you; and when you pass through the rivers, they will not sweep over you.
When you walk through the fire,
you will not be burned;
the flames will not set you ablaze."

Isaiah 43:2

We move a lot. I'm not sure I've ever talked to a woman who hasn't had to move at least once. The process of leaving always includes packing up countless boxes, filling up a giant U-Haul or at least several truck loads and discovering that you have a lot more stuff than you ever imagined!

Generally, the greater the distance of the move, the greater the unknown. A big move may include a new job, a new town, a new school, a new church, or even a new set of friends. It may include a new climate or a new culture! All that newness can stir up feelings of uncertainty.

Even little "moves" in life, like the move to a new career or promotion at work, the move to a new, deeper level of friendship, or the move to a new responsibility at church can raise the question *What's going to happen?* Any transition—no matter

how big or small—is usually accompanied by a fear of uncertainty. If left unchecked, that fear can take root in your life and eventually make you want to avoid change. You can become resistant to new things, and worse, resistant to the change God wants to do in your life, family, or community.

Whether you're entering a new stage in life, trying a new activity, meeting new people, moving to a new town, or starting a new job, there's probably a little fear that tugs at your heart strings. Though fear often accompanies the journey into the unknown, the truth is that God is bigger than any fear—including fear of failure.

Throughout the Bible, we read of men and women who responded to God's call on their lives. From Noah to Abraham to Mary, we read of men and women who were told to follow God into the unknown. They had to take risks in order to be obedient, but they never stepped forward alone. And when you step out in obedience, neither will you be alone. There will always be lots of "what ifs" in life, but God promises to be with you through every one.

1. What new "moves" or transitions has God recently led you through? What new "moves" or transitions do you feel God is calling you to right now?

2. On a scale of 1 to 10, how strong is the fear of the unknown during a time of transition for you? Does the fear ever slow or stop you from making the changes God is calling you to make in your life? If so, explain.

Throughout the Bible, we read of men and women who were called by God into the unknown. Undoubtedly, fear must have accompanied their journeys, but as we read their stories, we discover that their faith was stronger than any fear.

3. On the chart below, identify God's calling on each person's life and the result of their obedience despite any uncertainty or fear of the unknown.

Bible Passage	**What did God ask of the person?**	**What was the result of their obedience?**
Genesis 6:11–22, Genesis 8:14–22	build an ark w/ specs full	saved Noah, family & animals
Genesis 12:1–4, Hebrews 11:8–12	leave country, fam., go to new land	God est. Abe as a leader
Luke 1:26–38, Luke 2:6–7	have a child - Son of God name Jesus	M became mother of Jesus, Son of God

called to unknown, unexpected
great uncertainty, yet God was
faithful

Noah, Abraham and Mary are only three of a long list of people who followed God by faith. Take a moment and read Hebrews 11.

4. According to **Hebrews 11:1**, what is the definition of faith? Now rewrite this definition in your own words.

Faith is being sure (substance) of what is hoped for, evidence (certainty) (proof) of things unseen - all in your heart & mind

5. As you read **Hebrews 11:4–31**, what do you find to be most inspiring or encouraging about these individuals? Of those listed, who is most like a hero to you? Why?

6. Reflecting on **Hebrews 11:32–40**, how is your faith and the faith of others strengthened when you follow God into the unknown?

Looking at other's lives & faithfulness to God encourages us to be faithful, knowing He will fulfill His plans for us.

One of the great comforts you have in following God by faith wherever and however he may choose to lead you is that you do not go alone. God goes with you, but he also goes before you.

7. Read **Revelation 22:13**. What three phrases does God use to describe himself?

Alpha & Omega First & Last
Beginning & End

It's interesting to note that God describes himself as the *alpha* and the *omega*, the first and last letters of the Greek alphabet. The equivalent in English is to say God is the *A* and the *Z*. When some Jewish leaders translated this into their own language, they called God the *Aleph* and the *Tav*—the first and last letters of the Hebrew alphabet. But when referring to God, they went one step further and acknowledged him as the truth, which in Hebrew is spelled 'aleph-mem-tav—representing the first, middle, and last letters of the alphabet. Thus referring to God as the *'aleph-mem-tav* signifies that he is eternal and sovereign throughout time.

8. How does knowing that God goes before you strengthen your faith when it comes to facing the future?

The truth is that you can never know everything that will be around the next corner, but you can be assured that God and his promises will be there to greet you.

✦ Digging Deeper ✦

In the book of Esther, we read of a young woman facing highly uncertain times. When she discovers the plot to destroy the Jewish people, she must risk her own life in order to save herself and her people. Read Esther 4:13–17. Can you think of a "for such a time as this" moment in your own life? How was your response similar to Esther's? How was your response different?

✦ Ponder and Pray ✦

The opening Scripture for this lesson comes from Isaiah 43:2, and it reminds us, "When you pass through the waters, I will be with you; and when you pass through the rivers, they will not sweep over you. When you walk through the fire, you will not be burned; the flames will not set you ablaze." When fear about the "what ifs" grips our hearts, God wants to move our focus from what could happen to what he can do.

What "move" is God nudging you toward right now in your own life? In your faith? In your family? In your work?

✦ Notes & Prayer Requests ✦

Mary Jane & Jim
Jim Hamilton
Diane
Linda
Nancy & Shawn
Elijah
Ruthanne
Ida Austin
Amanda
So. border
Joann - pain
Joyce
country
children & grandchildren
Dick

Chapter 4

Facing the Fear of Rejection

"Peace I leave with you; my peace I give you. I do not give to you as the world gives. Do not let your hearts be troubled and do not be afraid."

John 14:27

Almost everyone receives a rejection letter at some point in her life. Most of us have received multiple rejections from a variety of sources—whether it's programs, schools, or jobs that turned us down. Undoubtedly, some of the rejection letters are harder to read than others.

But of all the rejection letters that life delivers, the most painful tend to come from people we care about, look up to, or love deeply. You see, it's one thing to have an institution turn you down, but it's another thing to have a friend reject you.

You may have reached out to a neighbor only to discover they were too busy to respond to your offer of friendship. You may have reached out to a coworker only to discover they wanted you to be just a fellow employee, not a friend. Or you may have tried to reach out to someone at church or a local community group only to discover that they didn't want to make time for you.

Such incidents can leave you feeling confused and rejected. And without realizing it, you can become a little wary of looking for opportunities to build new friendships and love others. If left unchecked, you may find fear of rejection springing up in your life. You may not want to reach out as much any more. Yet God calls you to reach out to others. God wants you to tear down any walls and begin trusting him and loving others again.

God calls us to move past any fear of rejection and into the full acceptance found in a relationship with him. Through Jesus, we can learn to love others in all of our relationships no matter what the response.

1. Reflecting on your own life, describe an incident when you experienced rejection. How did the incident affect you and your relationships with other people?

We read in Chapter One that fear played a significant role in the fall of man. Take a moment and reread **Genesis 3:1–13**.

2. What details in this passage suggest that Adam and Eve were afraid of being rejected by God? How did the fear of rejection affect their relationship with him?

sewed fig leaves-hid from God

3. Are there any ways in which you quietly fear rejection from God? If so, explain.

God wants you rooted in his love. He wants you to know and experience his love, whereby you may extend it to others.

4. Read the following verses and record what they reveal about God's love:

Jeremiah 31:3 everlasting love, drawn w/ loving-kindness, cont' faithfulness

John 13:1 J greatly loved His own, cont loves them with perfect love to the end

John 15:9 I have loved you just as F has loved me; remain in My love, do not doubt

Romans 8:35 Who shall ever separate us

1 John 3:1 See what an incredible quality of love the F has shown us that we are called the children of God

Take a few minutes to pray and ask God to make the truth of his love more real to you.

5. Read **Matthew 22:34–40**. When asked what is the single greatest commandment, Jesus actually responds by listing two. Why do you think he provided two commandments rather than just one? What are they?

So intimately linked
love of God = love of others

6. How do you think these two commands are linked or tied together? How can fear of rejection limit a person's ability to love God and love others?

When Jesus spoke of loving God and loving others in the Sermon on the Mount (Matt. 5–7), he never said that rejection would not come. Instead, he offered specific instructions on how to respond to those who reject you and treat you poorly.

7. Make a list of the things Jesus asks his followers to do in **Matthew 5:43–48.**

Love your enemies, pray for those who persecute you. Be perfect as God is perfect

What about Putin?

8. Reflecting on that list, is there anyone in your life whom you need to forgive, love, or pray for? How does loving your enemies set you free of any fear of rejection? Among those who have rejected you, who is God asking you to forgive, love, and pray for right now?

> *The truth is that, as a follower of Jesus, you will experience rejection, but it is not something to be feared. God wants your foundation built on him and his love, so that out of your relationship with him, you can love others—even those who reject you.*

✦Digging Deeper✦

Moses feared rejection from the very people God was sending him to lead. Read Exodus 4:1, 10. What specific issues fueled Moses's fear of rejection? Now read Exodus 4:1–12. How does God answer Moses's fear? What insight does this passage provide on how God answers our own fears when we face possible rejection?

✦ Ponder and Pray ✦

The opening Scripture for this lesson comes from John 14:27, where Jesus says, "Peace I leave with you; my peace I give you. I do not give to you as the world gives. Do not let your hearts be troubled and do not be afraid." Reflecting on your current relationships with friends, neighbors, coworkers, and family members, are there any areas where fear of rejection is holding you back from loving or serving others more? Ask God to uncover any weak spots in your relationships and begin his restoring work in your life.

✦ Notes & Prayer Requests ✦

✦ Notes & Prayer Requests ✦

CHAPTER 5

Conquering the Fear of Intimacy

"Now we see but a poor reflection
as in a mirror; then we shall see face to face.
Now I know in part; then I shall know fully,
even as I am fully known."

1 Corinthians 13:12

One of the most exciting things about relationships is that no two are exactly alike! Some relationships allow you to spend the afternoon chatting about anything and everything in life, while other relationships, like marriage, allow you to share the deepest parts of yourself with another.

In all of our relationships, we maintain a certain level of intimacy. We allow some people to get close—sharing our hopes, our dreams, and our innermost thoughts and prayers. But our relationships with others are a bit more distant. We may be content to only know a person's name or a few details about their life. In our interactions with these people, we keep things brief, vague, or on a surface level. As a result, we don't know them deeply and they don't know us. This inherently affects our communication in these relationships.

In *Secrets to Lasting Love*, Gary Smalley lists five levels of communication:

Level 1: Clichés. These are the routine comments and small talk delivered out of habit and include exchanges like, *"How are you?" "Good." "Nice day, isn't it?" "Sure is!"*

Level 2: Facts. These are the short conversations we engage in regarding the weather, work, common friends, news headlines, or weekend activities. These conversations don't require any real feeling or depth of thinking.

Level 3: Opinions. At this level, conversations become more personal, sharing hopes, dreams, desires, concerns, and even personal goals. At times, this level can get a little dicey as people share their differing perspectives on everything from life to politics.

Level 4: Feelings. Having overcome any differing perspectives, each person feels safe to share their deep emotions and how they really feel about things.

Level 5: Needs. This deepest level of communication is the most intimate and is most often found in a healthy marriage. You feel secure in revealing your needs with each other.

When you think about your relationships in these terms, you can see just how deep your communication goes with different people. You can begin to recognize the people you barely know—who maybe you exchange a Level 1 or 2 conversation with—compared to your closest friends or spouse, with whom you reach Levels 4 and 5.

So the question becomes, how many people *really* know you? How many people do you feel safe sharing your opinions, feelings, and even some of your needs with? Or does fear of getting too close hold you back from the meaningful relationships with which God wants to bless you?

1. What level of communication do you use with the majority of your friends? Do you tend to push your relationships to deeper or more surface levels of communication? Why?

2. Think of ten people you know. In the space below, write each person's first initial next to the level of communication you maintain with him or her.

Level of Communication	Person's First Initial
Level 1: Clichés	D, L, N, G
Level 2: Facts	D, E
Level 3: Opinions	G, Bs
Level 4: Feelings	N, A, Bs
Level 5: Needs	N, P, J

Does your list reveal anything about the levels of communication and intimacy you allow in your life?

When it comes to your relationship with God, he desires Level 5 communication with you! He wants an intimate relationship, where you can share your thoughts, your feelings, and your innermost needs through an ongoing conversation known as prayer. He does not want you to be fearful of intimacy, but to embrace a deeper relationship with him.

3. Read **Psalm 139:1–4** and **Psalm 139:13–15**. Reflecting on these verses, make a list of the things God knows about you. On a scale of one to ten, just how well does God really know you?

4. Knowing that God intimately knows you, does that make you want to push forward or pull away in your relationship with him? Why?

God knows you better than you know yourself. An intimate relationship with God is not to be feared but embraced! He knows your gifts, your strengths, and your beauty. He also knows your sins, your weaknesses, and the unattractive areas of your life. And he loves you anyway! His love for you is secure and unwavering.

5. Read **Revelation 3:20**. This verse paints a rich portrait of the relationship God desires with you. What does Jesus promise to do if you open the door to him in your life? Why do you think Jesus references sharing a meal with you? What kind of relationship does this imply?

eat with him (restore him

In the book of Acts, we read of the believers who were part of the first church. They shared their lives and their possessions with each other.

6. Read **Acts 2:42–46.** Like the passage in Revelation 3:20, there is a reference to sharing meals together. What other activities are listed? How do you think these activities brought the believers together and deepened their relationships?

shared possessions, learned tog, fellowship, prayers, awe, wonders & signs, selling & sharing, met in temple, unified, met in various homes, shared with joy & generosity

The truth is that, as a follower of Jesus, you are designed to be in healthy, intimate relationships with others.

7. Reflecting on the activities listed in **Acts 3:42–46**, which can you begin using right now to deepen your relationships?

8. Take a moment to think about the people God has placed in your life. Are there any people with whom you feel God nudging you to be more honest and open? Are there any friendships where your transparency can bring healing and hope?

✦ Digging Deeper ✦

Read 1 Kings 19:14–18. Elijah is on the run from Jezebel, and he is extremely discouraged. According to 1 Kings 19:14, what are Elijah's complaints before God? How does God answer those complaints in 1 Kings 19:15–18? What role does relationship—and the knowledge that you're not alone—play in God's kingdom? Why do you think it's so important that we don't isolate ourselves or fear intimate, close relationships with others?

✦ Ponder and Pray ✦

The opening Scripture for this lesson comes from 1 Corinthians 13:12, where Paul writes, "Now we see but a poor reflection as in a mirror; then we shall see face to face. Now I know in part; then I shall know fully, even as I am fully known." God calls us into authentic community with one another. We are designed to have people to share our hopes and dreams and needs with, even if it's just a few.

Are there any people from your past whom you were extremely close to that you've now lost track of? Is there anyone in your life right now whom God is calling you to reconnect with? Are there any people you need to write an email to, send a card to, or pick up the phone and call?

✦ Notes & Prayer Requests ✦

Free to Be Yourself

"We have different gifts, according to the grace given us."

Romans 12:6a

There's an often-told story of a young boy who walked the local beach looking for starfish. Whenever he found one of the little sea creatures, he would carefully pry its legs from any rocks before tossing it back into the sea. Under his careful watch, hundreds of starfish were returned to the water.

One day an older man noticed the young boy carefully throwing starfish back into the sea. Intrigued, he couldn't help but ask the boy about his ritual.

"Why do you throw the starfish back into the sea?" the old man asked.

"Because the starfish will die if left in the hot sun on the shore," the boy explained.

"But there are millions of starfish, and multitudes of shores with countless beaches upon which you will never walk," the man contended. "On each of those beaches there are throngs of starfish you will never save. Why do you bother?"

The boy looked down at the sand and picked up a starfish resting nearby.

"Because today, this day, this one will live," the boy replied. And he threw the starfish back into the sea.

The man watched as the boy continued his practice. Then, he reached down himself, picked up a starfish, and threw it into the sea.

The story is a rich reminder that in a world of needs, one person can make a big difference. It's also a lesson in the importance of doing what you are uniquely created, gifted, and called to do. Like so many others, the boy noticed the starfish dying on the seashore, but unlike the others, he made a decision to do something about it. He used the abilities God had given him to make a difference. Like the old man in the story, not everyone will always understand or get what you do, but regardless of the response, you are called to use the talents and gifts God has given you for his glory.

1. In the space below, make a list of five things you are naturally good at doing. Then, make a list of five things you are passionate about.

Your Gifts and Talents	**Your Passions and Interests**
(Example) Good at organizing	Caring for children
teaching	my family
encouraging	bible study
decorating	reading
mothering	

Now, take a moment and reflect on ways in which you can combine your gifts and talents with your passions and interests. In other words, how are you uniquely wired to make a difference in the world around you? (For example, encouraging friends to sponsor a child overseas after you sponsor one yourself.)

God designs every person differently. He gives us different personalities, different strengths and weaknesses, different gifts and talents. All of these differences can be used to help build his kingdom. In the Old Testament, God chose specific individuals with unique gifts to build the tabernacle.

2. Read **Exodus 31:1–11**. In the space below, make a list of the unique talents of Bezalel. artistic designs in gold, silver bronze, cut stones, wood carving.

What was Oholiab's role? help him

How did their gifts and placement compliment each other?

used gifts for building the tabernacle

Ch 25-30 desc.

35:30-39 repeats
34-35 taught others skills

3. Read **Exodus 36:1–2**. What qualities did the craftsman called by Moses need? Do you think it's possible to have one of those qualities and not the other? Explain. Why are they both important?

Sometimes fear can hold you back from using your talents, gifts, and even yourself to help others. You may be afraid of failure or afraid that you won't fit in or afraid that what you do won't really matter. But God makes it clear that everyone has a role to play in his kingdom.

4. Read 1 **Corinthians 12:4–26**. What will happen if one part of the body chooses not to function properly or shuts down completely? What will happen if one part of the body spends all its energy trying to pretend it's another part of the body? Why is it so crucial that every part of the body perform as it's uniquely designed?

5. Do you have any talents or gifts you're not using? Are there any areas in which you spend your time and energy trying to be someone you're not?

Jesus's Parable of the Talents offers a rich lesson on what it means to use what you're given—no matter how much or how little.

6. Read **Matthew 25:14–40**. What role did fear play in how the servant entrusted with one talent responded to his master? Why do you think the other two servants responded differently?

7. What is the message Jesus is trying to communicate through this parable? How does that message apply to your life right now?

It doesn't matter how much you've been given, but how you respond

8. Take a moment to feel your fingertips. Just as everyone's fingerprints are one-of-a-kind, so are our personalities, strengths, and contributions to the body of Christ. No one on the planet has the exact same blend of gifts, talents, and passion. Reflecting on the story of the boy and the starfish, who is God calling you to reach? Where is he calling you to make a difference right now?

The truth is that God has uniquely created, gifted, and called you to service in his kingdom.

✦DIGGING DEEPER✦

Sometimes when we step out in faith and use our talents and gifts for good and for God's glory, things don't always go according to plan.

Read Galatians 5:7–8. How do you respond to those who are trying to discourage you from fulfilling the call on your life? What steps do you need to take to surround yourself with people who will encourage you, challenge you, and pray for you?

✦PONDER AND PRAY✦

The opening Scripture for this lesson comes from Romans 12:6a where Paul writes, "We have different gifts, according to the grace given us."

Take a few moments to reflect on your life so far. Are there any talents or gifts that you used in an earlier age or stage of life that you've packed up and put away? Do you have a gift for music or art or math or science or any other that you haven't been using? What steps do you need to take to begin using that gift once again? How can it be used to bless and encourage others?

✦ Notes & Prayer Requests ✦

Fear of Lack— God as Provider

"Do not be anxious about anything, but in everything, by prayer and petition, with thanksgiving, present your requests to God."

Philippians 4:6

Almost every woman has experienced financial strain at some point in her life. It takes all kinds of forms. You may have struggled to launch out on your own—as a recent graduate or an entrepreneur. You may have tried to buy a house and realized you didn't have the money you needed for the down-payment. You may have found yourself suddenly burdened by overwhelming debt. Or maybe you or your spouse lost a much-needed job.

Even right now, you may have reached the point (or have recently been at the point) where you were or are about to lose everything. There's nothing to hold onto. Or is there?

Whether you have lost everything or you feel like you're about to lose everything, the truth is that you cannot lose God. He was with you before the loss, and he will be with you through the loss and after the loss. He will be with you through the frustration, the exhaustion, and the disappointment. And along the way, he invites you to know him as your provider.

Though the fear of lack is great, God's provision is always greater. Your needs do not escape his notice. All of us will face a fear of lack sometime in our lives—whether it's a lack of food, money, relationships, good health, or the basic provisions needed. No matter your income bracket, no one is immune to the fear of not having enough. But God is greater than any fear and he answers our fear of lack with an invitation to faith that he is more than enough. When you turn to him in prayer, you can't help but discover the power of his provision in your life.

1. Think of a time when you were in great need. Did you take your need to God through prayer? If so, how did he respond? How did things turn out? How did you learn or grow through the experience?

Throughout Scripture, we find God often described as a shepherd. He is One who provides, protects, and leads his sheep. One of the best portraits of the work of God as a shepherd is found in Psalm 23.

2. Take a moment to read **Psalm 23**, then in the space below, record all the activities described. Once you record the activities, go back and circle the verbs or action words in your notes.

Example: Makes me lie down.

makes, leads, restores, guides
comforts, prepares, anoints

Notice how active God is in your life! The psalm opens with the line, "The Lord is my shepherd, I shall not be in want" (Ps. 23:1). Then, the passage goes on to show the many ways God is providing for us through his guidance, leadership, restoration, protection, comfort, blessing, and assurance. The truth is that God's provision in our lives takes many different forms—and not just financial ones.

3. In what ways have you seen God, as described in Psalm 23, provide for you and your family?

In 1 Kings 17, we read two powerful stories of God as provider back-to-back. The prophet, Elijah, is in need of food and God provides for him in two miraculous but very different ways.

4. Read **1 Kings 17:1–6** and **1 Kings 17:7–16**. How did God supply food to Elijah in each situation?

ravens

woman & son

Recognizing that God could have continued to feed Elijah using the ravens, why do you think God told Elijah to go to the widow? How did Elijah's lack of food become a source of provision for the widow and her family?

In the New Testament, we read of another woman who was in great need. We know that she lacked because she is described as a "poor widow." In the ancient world, widows lived in cultural context where they were more likely to be financially needy, with no one to care for them.

5. Read **Mark 12:41–46**. Though the passage does not say, what do you think motivated the poor widow to make her offering? Do you think that this woman had a fear of lack? Why or why not? What was the result of her generous gift?

6. Like the widow, have you ever given out of your lack rather than out of your abundance? What was the result? How did you experience God as provider in the situation?

In the Sermon on the Mount, Jesus makes it clear that he does not want you to fear any sort of lack, but rather he invites you to live by faith.

7. Read **Matthew 6:25–34**. What kind of lack—financial, relational, etc.—are you most likely to fear? What verse in this passage offers the most comfort or encouragement to you regarding that fear?

8. Is there any fear of lack that you can identify in your life right now? What is holding you back from handing that fear over to God and trusting that he will provide?

The truth is that God is greater than any fear of lack you may have. When you turn to him in prayer, you discover the power of his provision in your life.

✦DIGGING DEEPER✦

Read Luke 12:32–34. In this passage, Jesus once again steers our hearts away from fear of "lack." Why do you think Jesus makes this message so clear? What does a fear of lack in your life reveal about your faith in God as provider? What does fear of lack in your life reveal about where your true treasure rests (Luke 12:34)?

✦PONDER AND PRAY✦

The opening Scripture for this lesson comes from Philippians 4:6, where Paul writes, "Do not be anxious about anything, but in everything, by prayer and petition, with thanksgiving, present your requests to God." Little fears of lack can come into our lives at any time, but we're particularly susceptible to them during times of transition. Whether you're moving to a new job, a new location, or a new stage of life, you may wonder *Is God going to provide?* What does Paul encourage us to do when faced with anxiety? What prayers, petitions, and thanksgivings do you want to offer right now?

✦ Notes & Prayer Requests ✦

CHAPTER 8

Fear of Loss— God as Protector

"In God I trust; I will not be afraid. What can man do to me?"

Psalm 56:11

Almost every important date in history is known by the month, the day, and the year, but when it comes to September 11, those two words are enough. That was the day when everything in our country changed in an instant. Thousands of lives were lost. Millions of people were stranded. And almost everyone felt a sense of loss. Not just a tremendous loss of life, but also a loss of life as we knew it.

All of us will experience moments in life when everything changes. A family member dies. A loved one is diagnosed with an incurable disease. An accident leaves you or someone you care about injured. A sudden cutback and layoff at work leaves you unemployed.

Such moments remind us that life can change in any moment and the things we love, enjoy, or need can be taken away.

A few years ago, my health suddenly started deteriorating. I was tired, weak, and experiencing phenomenal abdominal pain. When I couldn't walk up the steps in my home, I knew it was time to see a doctor. I was quickly scheduled for surgery, but even after the procedure, my health didn't return immediately.

During that time, I felt a tremendous sense of loss. I lost my energy, my ability to enjoy food, and my ability to build relationships and enjoy life, because there were many days when I could barely get out of bed. And I quietly wondered, *Would things ever go back to the way they used to be?* I prayed a lot, and among so many unanswered questions, the one thing I knew for sure was that God had not left me. Even in the sickness, he was still my protector.

I suffered with pain and relapses until slowly the doctors and I developed a program to manage my health condition largely through diet, exercise, and rest. Though the life as I knew it was taken away, I have found God replacing it with a fuller life—one that is more balanced and restful.

The truth is that God calls us to trust him with all things—including the possibility of loss. But even if something is taken away from your life, God is faithful to protect you, guide you, and see you through.

1. Reflecting on your own life, think of a personal loss. How did God make himself real to you through that experience? How did God reveal himself to you as your protector through the experience?

2. What would be the hardest single thing for you to lose in your life right now? Do you believe that God could protect and provide for you even if you lost that one thing? Why or why not?

In the book of Ruth we read of some women who experienced tremendous loss. Naomi married Elimelech, and together they had two sons. But then Elimelech died, and she was left a widow. Eventually, one of her sons married a woman named Ruth, and the other son married a woman named Orpah. But then, both sons died. Naomi, Ruth, and Orpah were all widows together. That's when Naomi made the decision to return to her homeland. She knew it wasn't fair to ask her widowed daughters-in-law to go with her, so she encouraged them to go back to their own families.

3. Read **Ruth 1:6–18**. What motivated Naomi to risk further loss—the loss of relationship with her daughters-in-law (Ruth 1:8–9)? What was the result of her actions (Ruth 1:16–18)?

They could remarry. As a result of her actions, Ruth chose to stay with her & adopt her country and her God.

Naomi and Ruth traveled to Bethlehem together at the beginning of the barley harvest. While there, Ruth found favor with a wealthy kinsman named Boaz, whom she eventually married. As a result, Ruth became the great-grandmother of David—an ancestor in the line of Jesus. Through this story, we discover that no matter what hardship or loss a person goes through, nothing is beyond God's redemption.

One of the most remarkable stories of personal loss is found in the life story of Job. Described as a man who was blameless, upright, fearing God and turning away from evil, Job suffered indescribable loss as God allowed Satan to test him.

4. Read **Job 1:13–19**. Make a list of things Job lost within this passage.

oxen, donkeys, servants, sheep, camels, sons & daughters

5. Read **Job 1:20–22**. What can we learn from Job about how to respond to loss in our lives?

Mourned, then blessed the Lord.
Recognized that all things came from Lord - weren't his own
Didn't sin by blaming Lord.

6. Read **Philippians 3:~~8~~7–11**. What did the apostle Paul gain through his losses? Knowledge of Christ

7. How can the losses of this life bring us closer to Jesus? Do you think it's possible for losses to teach us things about God we could never learn otherwise? Explain.

8. What words of encouragement have you been able to extend to others because of the losses you've experienced in your life?

The truth is that God calls you to trust him with all things—including the possibility of loss. He is your perfect Provider.

✦Digging Deeper✦

In the previous lesson we studied the story of the widow at Zarepeth who had run out of food and experienced God's miraculous provision. But the story doesn't end there. God also protected her from loss. Read 1 Kings 17:17–24. What demand does Elijah make of the widow in verse 19? What is the result of the widow handing over her son? Do you think God ever asks us to hand over losses to him? If so, what does he do with them? What losses is God asking you to hand over to him right now?

✦Ponder and Pray✦

The opening Scripture for this lesson comes from Psalm 56:11, "In God I trust; I will not be afraid. What can man do to me?" When we put our faith in God, fear of loss has no grip on us. We begin to recognize God as our protector not just of what we have but even what we don't have.

Think of someone you know who has recently experienced a significant loss. Pray for them, and ask God how you can be a voice of encouragement, love, and grace in their life.

✦ Notes & Prayer Requests ✦

Fear of Death—God as Redeemer

"The Lord will rescue me from every evil attack and will bring me safely to his heavenly kingdom. To him be glory for ever and ever. Amen."

2 Timothy 4:18

It's no secret that our broken places can become a source of strength and life to others. Consider author and speaker, Barbara Johnson, who survived incredibly devastating experiences, including the death of her two sons—one in Vietnam and the other by a drunk driver. Meanwhile, her third son disappeared into the homosexual lifestyle for many years until a profound moment of reconciliation brought them together again. More recently, she has had to face a malignant brain tumor and the loss of her husband.

Yet in the face of so much death, God has brought new life not only into her heart but into the hearts of millions of others. Through her speaking and writing, she has become a source of inspiration and encouragement to countless people who have faced unbelievable challenges.

Death is never easy, and yet it's something no one can avoid. Not only do we face physical death—both for ourselves and those we love—but we must also face the death of our dreams when things just don't turn out the way we expect. It's in these

moments that we discover God not just as a source of life but as our Redeemer. No situation is too difficult for him to handle. Nothing is beyond his redeeming power.

As a believer, death has no hold on you or your dreams, and God has promised you not only a purpose but a new home that's beyond your imagination.

1. Have you ever had something you really wanted but finally had to give up on? Have you ever had a dream die? If so, explain. How did things turn out?

2. At some point, we will all experience a physical death. What is your greatest fear about death or the process of dying?

Even in death, God is with you. Knowing God as your Redeemer can fill you with faith and hope. The words of Job become powerful words of comfort no matter what happens. Job 19:25–26 says, "I know that my Redeemer lives, and that in the end he will stand upon the earth. And after my skin has been destroyed, yet in my flesh I will see God."

Through Jesus, death has no hold on us! As **Romans 6:23** says, "For the wages of sin is death, but the gift of God is eternal life in Christ Jesus our Lord." When you choose to make Jesus the center of your life and accept him as your Savior, death can have no hold on you. Even in physical death, God promises to bring you to a new eternal life with him.

3. On the chart below, draw lines connecting the verses with God as our Redeemer even in death.

Bible Passage	What Is God's Promise?
Psalm 48:14	Even in death the righteous have a refuge.
Psalm 49:15	Everyone who believes in Jesus will have eternal life.
Psalm 73:26	He will be your guide even to the end.
Proverbs 14:32	He will redeem your life and take you to himself.
John 3:15	God is the strength of your heart and your portion forever.

Which of these Scriptures is the most comforting to you? Why? Is there anything stopping you from choosing to follow Jesus and make him the center of your life?

4. Read **John 12:23–25**. What do you think Jesus meant when he said, "Unless a kernel of wheat falls to the ground and dies, it remains only a single seed." What things can you think of that have to die in order to come to new life?

foretold his death, plants & trees – leaves die in Fall. New life in Spring. We die to old self – born again

5. In John 15, Jesus describes himself as a vine and the Father as a gardener. Read **John 15:1–4**. Do you see any parallels between the process that happens to wheat when it falls to the ground and the process of a branch being pruned? Explain.

Both involve a type of death

6. Have you ever experienced a death or "pruning" that resulted in new life? Describe.

In the book of Daniel, we read of King Nebuchadnezzar, who set a decree that whenever music was played everyone in the land had to fall down and worship a ninety-foot-tall gold statue. Whoever did not fall down and worship the statue would face certain death in a fiery furnace. Three Jews refused to bow and were brought before the king.

7. Read Daniel 3:13–30. What was the testimony Shadrach, Meshach, and Abednego were able to give in Daniel 3:17–18 because they chose faith in God over fear of death? How was God able to redeem the situation as a result of their faith-filled declaration (Daniel 3:28–29)?

8. Reflecting on your own life's situation, what opportunities are present for you to be faith-filled? What God-infused declarations do you need to make in your life right now?

The truth is that as a follower of Jesus, death has no hold on you.

✦ Digging Deeper ✦

Tucked into Psalm 116 is an often overlooked verse. Read Psalm 116:15. Why do you think the death of the saints would be described as "precious" to the Lord? How is God's perspective on death different from your own? What steps do you need to take to share God's perspective on death?

✦ Ponder and Pray ✦

The opening Scripture for this lesson comes from 2 Timothy 4:18, "The Lord will rescue me from every evil attack and will bring me safely to his heavenly kingdom. To him be glory for ever and ever. Amen." In what areas of your life do you feel under "attack"? What situations in your life right now need God's redeeming power? Take a moment to pray about each one, asking God for his grace, strength, peace, and mighty hand in those situations.

✦ Notes & Prayer Requests ✦

✦ Notes & Prayer Requests ✦

CHAPTER 10

EMBRACING HIS LOVE

"THERE IS NO FEAR IN LOVE.
BUT PERFECT LOVE DRIVES OUT FEAR,
BECAUSE FEAR HAS TO DO WITH PUNISHMENT.
THE ONE WHO FEARS IS NOT MADE PERFECT IN LOVE."

1 John 4:18

How's my relationship with my dad? It's one of the simplest but most powerful questions you can ever ask yourself, because your relationship with your dad can affect your relationship with God. If your earthly dad is kind and generous and makes lots of time for you, then you're more likely to see God, your heavenly Father, as kind, generous, and always there for you.

Unfortunately, not everyone has such healthy encounters with their earthly fathers. For some, their dads were abusive. For others, they were simply not around. Such experiences with our earthly fathers can affect the way we understand and respond to our heavenly Father. You may see God as abusive or even absent. You may have an unhealthy fear of him, or worse, think he does not care at all.

That's why it's so important to know what the Bible says about God. In his Word, we find the truth of who he is. We find the balance of loving him and yet also having a healthy fear of

him. We discover his kindness and love. And in Jesus, we are given a vivid portrait of his heart toward us.

The truth is that an unhealthy understanding of God can hold you back from a real relationship with him. God disciplines those he loves, but it always has a purpose—to make you more like himself. While a great godly dad can reflect God's image, no earthly father can ever compare to the holiness of God.

We serve a God who promises to gives us more than we ask for. He lavishes us with his love. And he invites us into a relationship with him that is more rewarding than we could ever expect.

1. How has your relationship with your earthly father affected your understanding of your heavenly Father?

2. In what ways did your dad reflect God's character to you?

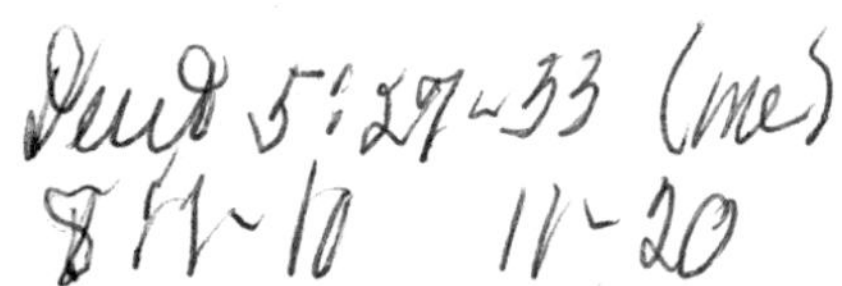

3. Read **Deuteronomy 8**. What does God require of his people? How does God promise to provide for his people? How would you describe God's promise of provision (stingy, abundant, etc.)?

observe God's commands, walk in His way, revere Him, Praise Him & not forget Him, thinking we did it all on our own, without Him.
God provides a rich land with plenty of water, food & precious metals. God's provision is richly abundant.

4. Reflecting on this chapter, what is the purpose of God's discipline? How do you learn or grow through discipline?

Disciplines us with His love to get us back into a relationship with Him

5. Read **Hebrews 12:1–11**. Why is God's discipline good for us? How do we benefit? Can you think of a moment when God has disciplined you? What was the result?

share in His holiness. Make us more like Christ. Yields the peaceful fruit of righteousness & peace
proves He is a good father & we are true children
2 Peter 1:2-8

Even when you sin or fall short of God's best for your life, his love remains steadfast. Peter, one of Jesus's disciples, experienced this love firsthand.

6. Read **Mark 14:66–72**. What kind of response do you think Peter expected from Jesus after his repeated denial?

rebuke, discipline

John 21:15-17

16:9-13

7. Read **Mark 16:14–20**. What kind of response did Peter, along with the other disciples who also doubted that he had risen from the dead, actually get from Jesus? What did Jesus command them to do? How did they respond?

rebuked disciples for lack of faith and stubborn refusal to believe. Sent them on Great Commission. They obeyed

8. A healthy understanding of the fear of God will motivate us to obey God and follow his commands, which inherently will lead us to live our best possible life. Are there any areas in your life where an unhealthy fear of God is limiting your relationship with him? Are there any areas in your life where an unhealthy understanding of God is limiting your willingness to obey him?

The truth is that a healthy fear and understanding of God will push you toward a deeper relationship with him.

✦Digging Deeper✦

John 21 goes into greater detail about one of Peter's first interactions with Jesus after he denied him. Read John 21:7–9. How did Peter respond to the news that Jesus was on the shore? How did this response compare to that of the other disciples? Now read John 21:15–19. What did Jesus do to reinstate Peter and remind him of Jesus's great love for him? Even after the denials, did Jesus's love for Peter change in any way? Did his calling change? What does this passage reveal about God's all-embracing love?

✦Ponder and Pray✦

The opening Scripture for this lesson comes from 1 John 4:18, "There is no fear in love. But perfect love drives out fear, because fear has to do with punishment. The one who fears is not made perfect in love." Reflecting on your life, in what ways has God been making you "perfect in love"? What has that process looked like in your life? How is God changing you to make you look more like himself?

✦ Notes & Prayer Requests ✦

CHAPTER 11

Sharing Your Faith

"But even if you should suffer for what is right, you are blessed. 'Do not fear what they fear; do not be frightened.' But in your hearts set apart Christ as Lord. Always be prepared to give an answer to everyone who asks you to give the reason for the hope that you have."

1 Peter 3:14–15a

On a recent airline flight, I found myself sitting next to a middle-aged man. I decided to strike up a conversation with him. When I asked him where he was going, he said, "I'm going to get my daughters."

The seriousness of his voice piqued my interest; I wanted to know more. He explained that his daughters were living with his ex-wife, but now they were in an abusive situation, and he was going to get them and bring them home where they would be safe.

I knew I needed to pray *with* the man, not just *for* the man. During the rest of the flight, I couldn't shake the feeling that he needed someone to reach out and verbally pray with him, but I never did it. I was too afraid. When the plane landed, I looked at the man and said, "God bless you" and offered up a series of silent prayers for him. I know God heard those prayers, but it wasn't the same as if I actually obeyed God in the moment. I repented, and promised that if given the same opportunity again, I wouldn't miss it.

Sometime later, I was on another flight and struck up a conversation with the person next to me. Again, I felt an unmistakable urge, but this time it was simply to ask the person if he went to church. I took a big gulp and asked the simple question. It turns out the man's wife had been trying to convince him to go to church, but he wasn't sure about it. For the rest of the flight we talked about God and issues of faith. Every so often the man would stop and ask, "Why did you ask me that question about church? No one besides my wife has talked to me about spiritual issues in years."

I smiled and thanked God for the opportunity.

Though I am passionate about Jesus and have been following him for many years, I still get a little scared when it comes to sharing my faith. There's always a moment when I have to take a deep breath and decide whether or not I'm going to take the plunge off the diving board of faith into a conversation about Jesus with others. Yet every time I do it, I find that I am richly rewarded—not only by the depth of the conversations, but also by the strengthening of my own faith.

No matter what fears you may have about sharing your faith, you can overcome them. God wants to take your fear and replace it with a greater faith in him and his ways. He wants to use you to spread the good news of Jesus!

1. Are you ever apprehensive about sharing your faith? If so, what is the root cause of the fear?

2. Think of a time when you shared your faith with someone else. What was the result? How did you feel afterward?

3. People come to know Jesus in many different ways. There is no cookie-cutter approach when it comes to God. Read **John 1:35–50**. In the space below, record how each disciple found out about Jesus.

Andrew: through John the Baptist

Simon (Peter): through Andrew

Philip: called by Jesus to follow Him

Nathaniel: told by Philip

Reflecting on this passage, why do you think it's so important to verbally tell others about Jesus? What does it mean to introduce someone to Jesus?

4. Read **Matthew 28:16–20**. What are the key elements of the Great Commission? Which element of the Great Commission are you least comfortable practicing?

All authority given to Him in Heaven & on earth (sovereign). Go therefore & make disciples of all nations, baptizing them in the name of the Father, Son & Holy Ghost teaching His commands. I am with you always to the end of the age.

5. How does fear prevent you from fulfilling the Great Commission? Explain. How is God calling you to move beyond your fear and live by faith in this area in your life?

Sharing your faith does not need to be forced or manufactured. It can begin with the simplest of conversations, an offer to pray with someone, an encouraging note, or mentioning a Scripture. Sharing your faith can be as easy as telling what God has done in your life.

6. In the space below, make a list of three ways God has made himself real to you.

The truth is that no matter the fears you may have about sharing your faith, you can overcome them with God's strength.

7. Now, list three things God has done in your life.

8. In the next week look for someone with whom you can share something from your lists. It can be a stranger, a friend, or a neighbor. But look for someone to engage in a spiritual conversation. Share your experience with your discussion group!

✦Digging Deeper✦

Read Romans 3:23, Romans 10:8–9, Luke 24:46–47, and John 1:11. How can these Scriptures help you share and express your own faith to others? Which of these do you want to commit to memory for the next time you have the opportunity to share your faith?

✦Ponder and Pray✦

The opening Scripture for this lesson comes from 1 Peter 3:14–16, "But even if you should suffer for what is right, you are blessed. 'Do not fear what they fear; do not be frightened.' But in your hearts set apart Christ as Lord. Always be prepared to give an answer to everyone who asks you to give the reason for the hope that you have." What does Peter suggest we focus on when we find ourselves fearful of sharing our faith? Take a moment to reflect on "the hope that you have." Write a few sentences defining that hope in your own life. Ask God to make that hope contagious so others will ask you about it.

✦ Notes & Prayer Requests ✦

Trusting God with All the Details

"Have I not commanded you?
Be strong and courageous. Do not be terrified;
do not be discouraged, for the Lord your God
will be with you wherever you go."

Joshua 1:9

The disciples were flabbergasted. After following Jesus for three years, they had the opportunity to see countless miracles performed right before their eyes. They watched as blind eyes were opened, deaf ears were restored, the lame took their first steps, and people were restored to a right relationship with God. Then, they watched as Jesus was brutally killed on a cross. Three days later he came back to life, and now he was leaving them again.

They watched yet another miracle—his ascension—and undoubtedly stood afterward in silence, staring into the sky. His final words were a powerful commission. The disciples were to take the message of Jesus to the ends of the earth. Can you imagine the weight of that responsibility? The presence of self-doubt? How could this ragamuffin band of disciples possibly take the good news of Jesus to all people?

Yet in the book of Acts we find them gathered in one room doing the most powerful thing they knew to do: praying. Not only did God hear their prayers, but he also responded. And within a few days of going out and sharing the good news of Jesus—thousands began to believe in him. Today, we still see the impact of the original followers of Jesus all around us—in churches, homes, and families—where people are still spreading the news of him.

When God calls us to do something, he doesn't just want us to trust him with the big issues but also with all the details. Nothing escapes his notice. Nothing is too small for him.

The God who knows the number of the hairs on our heads (Matt. 10:30) has it all under control—even when we don't. Fear and anxiety can serve as signposts of areas where we don't trust God or turn to him first. Sometimes we give something over to God through prayer, but then we take it back. Or worse, we hold back certain areas from him entirely.

No matter what God is calling you to do—in ministry, your community, your church, or your family—God invites you to trust him with everything. Remember, he takes care of the big picture as well as the smallest details.

1. Have you ever given something over to God through prayer and then taken it back? Describe the experience.

2. Are there any things that you consider too small for God to worry about? What are they? How big must something be before it becomes God's concern?

3. Read **Luke 1:26–38**. Make a list of things that Mary could have feared. How did she respond instead?

Could have feared angel's message, rejection by Joseph, family, community.

4. Read **Luke 1:46–55**. What is the focus of Mary's response? What does Mary's response to God in the midst of so much change reveal about what your response should be during times of uncertainty?

focused on God. He is source of strength & hope & worship

5. Read **Matthew 21:1–9**. What circumstances had to be just right in order to provide Jesus with a donkey colt?

just as Jesus predicted with donkey, colt, person willing to give him up

6. It's easy to think that God doesn't care about the details, but in this story we read that he takes care of all the details. Why was this detail of the donkey colt so important for this stage in Jesus's ministry?

fulfilled a prediction

7. If God can take care of providing a donkey for the disciples to bring to Jesus, is there anything that is too small for him? What "donkey colts," or small things, have you seen God provide for you?

8. Are there any details in your life causing you fear or anxiety that you have not taken to God in prayer? What's stopping you from giving them to him?

The truth is that God takes care of the big picture and the smallest details! With him, you have nothing to fear.

✦Digging Deeper✦

Read Matthew 8:23–27. What is the disciples' response to the storm? How does this compare to Jesus's response to the storm? How do you tend to respond to the storms in your own life?

✦Ponder and Pray✦

The opening Scripture for this lesson comes from Joshua 1:9, "Have I not commanded you? Be strong and courageous. Do not be terrified; do not be discouraged, for the Lord your God will be with you wherever you go." Why do you think God commands us to be "strong and courageous"? What is the source of our strength and courage? Is there any place you can go where God will not go with you? Take a few minutes and commit this Scripture to memory. Look for ways in the upcoming week to use it as a prayer.

✦ Notes & Prayer Requests ✦

✦LEADER'S GUIDE✦

Each chapter begins with an illustration and an icebreaker question intended to help the women in your group relax and join in the discussion. There isn't a "right" answer to any of these warm-up questions, so everyone can participate without fear of giving a wrong response. Try to include everyone in this part of the discussion to help the group feel comfortable and become involved in the subject matter.

Eight discussion questions guide you through the content of the chapter. When you pose one of these questions, be sure to give your group plenty of time to think. Don't be surprised if they grow silent temporarily. This is fairly common in discussion groups, and the leader who gives the group ample time to reflect will find they will open up and talk. To help you stay on track, this guide identifies questions intended to draw out opinions and provides information for questions aimed at more specific answers.

The highlighted box in the study states the main point of the chapter and corresponds to the **Focus** in the guide.

Digging Deeper is for those who want to do more thinking or digging in God's Word. This part is optional for discussion, but we hope you will want to go a little deeper in your study.

Ponder and Pray offers a great way to wrap up your study by reflecting on the opening Scripture. It's an opportunity for additional reflection and prayer.

Chapter 1: Outside My Comfort Zone

Focus: While some fear is healthy and serves as means of protection, unhealthy fear can hold you back in your life and relationships and prevent you from experiencing all God has for you. God does not want you to be controlled by unhealthy fears, anxieties, or phobias. He wants you to trust him with everything!

1, 2. These initial questions are designed as icebreakers to help you identify some of the fears that people often face. The responses from the group should be a reminder that no one is immune from fear—everyone struggles with fear on some level.

3. Psalm 91:5–10 mentions the terror of night, arrow that flies by day, pestilence that stalks in the darkness, and plague that destroys at midday. Some modern equivalents might include nightmares, wars, tension in the Middle East (including Afghanistan), terrorism, as well as threats such as the Ebola virus, bird flu, and mad cow disease. Encourage participants to pull responses from the latest news headlines to show that even after thousands of years, God's promise to protect us from these things still remains the same.

4. God promises his protection if we make him our dwelling and our refuge.

5. Fear causes Adam to hide. Some may interpret this as a sign of Adam pulling back from his relationship with God. Fear also contributes to Adam's blaming Eve. The lesson here is that fear undermines healthy relationships with God and others.

6. Sarah lies. The lesson here is that fear can cause us to commit a wide range of other sins, including lying.

7. Fear would hold back the Israelites from defeating the people of the land they were to occupy. The lesson here is that fear can keep us from experiencing God's best for our lives.

8. This is a more intimate personal-reflection question. Participants may or may not feel comfortable sharing their responses.

✦Digging Deeper✦

Laban's complaint is that Jacob deceived him and snuck away with his daughters without telling him. Laban complains he didn't even have the opportunity to throw a celebration or kiss his family members good-bye. Jacob lists fear as the core issue behind his secret departure.

Chapter 2: Letting Go of the Past

Focus: Sometimes experiences from our past open up the doorway to unhealthy fears in our lives. God wants to heal us, restore us, and rebuild our foundation on him.

1. This icebreaker question challenges participants to reflect on their pasts and identify any specific moments where fear took root in their lives.

2, 3. These questions ask participants to reflect on how an unhealthy personal fear can be passed on to others including children, friends, and family members.

4. God describes himself as Israel's King, Redeemer, Lord Almighty, the First, the Last, and a Rock. These descriptions remind us that God is all-powerful, sovereign, stable, and strong.

5. A rock is solid, stable, firm, and worthy for building a foundation on. Experiences from our pasts are unstable, shifting, and uncertain, whereas God is the Rock that holds true.

6. David turns a potential fear-filling experience into an opportunity to discover God's power and protection. He remembered God's faithfulness and used it as a springboard for the courage he needed to take on the Philistine.

7, 8. These introspective questions are designed to allow participants to seek God for the areas he wants to heal, restore, and use to build faith in others.

✦Digging Deeper✦

Invite participants to share the Scripture that they've memorized and what it specifically means to them. Find out how God has used this Scripture in their life in the past week.

Chapter 3: Running Toward the Future

Focus: Change is never easy, but God wants us to walk into the future with expectation and hope knowing that the God who goes with us also goes before us.

1. This icebreaker question challenges participants to reflect on their pasts and presents and to identify any specific situations where God has brought them into places of transition.

2. Participants who struggle more with change and new experiences will rank higher on the scale of 1 to 10.

3.

Bible Passage	What was asked of the person?	What was the result of the person's obedience?
Genesis 6:11–22, Genesis 8:14–22	Build an ark with specific dimensions and fill it with his family and living creatures.	God preserved Noah's family and all the living creatures on the ark. God established a covenant never to destroy all living creatures again.
Genesis 12:1–4, Hebrews 11:8–12	Leave your country, your people, and your extended family and go to a new land.	God established Abraham as a spiritual father and a leader of those who have looked for a city whose architect and builder is God.
Luke 1:26–38, Luke 2:6–7	Have a child, the Son of God, and name him Jesus.	Mary became the mother of Jesus, the Son of God.

It's interesting to note that Noah, Abraham, and Mary were all called to something that was much bigger than they were. They were called to the unexpected, the unknown, and great uncertainty. Yet God was faithful to them.

4. Faith is being sure of what we hope for and certain of what we do not see. Personal definitions will vary.

5. Answers will vary among participants.

6. Answers will vary, but one of the ways our faith and the faith of others is strengthened is through watching people follow God for their entire lives. We see their testimony, the fruit of their lives, and their faith, and it encourages us to be faithful ourselves—no matter what the cost.

7. Alpha and Omega. The First and the Last. The Beginning and the End.

8. Answers will vary among participants.

✦Digging Deeper✦

As participants share their "for such a time as this" moments, look for common threads or themes. How has God been faithful during these times?

Chapter 4: Facing the Fear of Rejection

Focus: God calls us to move past any fear of rejection into the full acceptance and love found in a right relationship with him. He wants to be our foundation in everything.

1. This icebreaker question challenges participants to reflect on their pasts and presents and to identify any specific situations where they have experienced rejection.

2. They sewed fig leaves and hid from God.

3. Answers will vary, but some participants may quietly fear that God doesn't love them or only loves them on a conditional basis.

4.
- Jeremiah 31:3: God's love is everlasting. He draws us to himself with his loving-kindness.
- John 13:1: Jesus showed us the full extent of God's love through his sacrifice.
- John 15:9: Jesus wants us to remain in God's love.
- Romans 8:35: Nothing can separate us from God's love.
- 1 John 3:1: God lavishes us with his love. He goes so far as to call us his children.

5. The reason for Jesus's response is debatable, but it can be argued that he listed the two commands—to love the Lord your God with all your heart and with all your soul and with all your mind and to love your neighbor as yourself—because they are so intimately linked. When we love God with our whole being, we cannot help but love others.

6. See response to Question 5. Fear of rejection from God can prevent us from drawing near to him, and fear of rejection from others can prevent us from extending his love. Thus, fear of rejection can impede our ability to fulfill the two greatest commands.

7. Love your enemies. Pray for those who persecute you. Be perfect like God.

8. This is a more intimate personal-reflection question. Participants may or may not feel comfortable sharing their responses.

✦ Digging Deeper ✦

Moses was afraid the people would reject him by not believing or listening to him. He argued that his lack of eloquence and slow speech would impede his ability to find acceptance among the people. God responded to Moses's fear with tangible, miraculous signs of his presence. God uses the staff, the leprosy, and the water to remind Moses (and the people) of his power. In essence, God responds to Moses's fear with an invitation of faith. Yet Moses still questions God (Exod. 4:10). That's when God reminds Moses that he is the all-powerful Creator. Nothing—including Moses's speech impediment—escapes God's notice. There are several take-away lessons, including the fact that God calls us, loves us, and plans to use us despite our "slow" areas. In addition, God reminded Moses that he is more powerful than any obstacle or fear. He is the God we should put our faith in no matter what we're facing.

Chapter 5: Conquering the Fear of Intimacy

Focus: God calls us into relationship with one another whereby we can be blessed and a blessing to others.

1. This icebreaker question challenges participants to reflect on their relationships and levels of communication and intimacy with others.

2. This is a more intimate personal-reflection question. Participants may or may not feel comfortable sharing their responses.

3. God knows when we sit, when we rise, and our innermost thoughts. God knows what we're thinking before we even say it. God knows our innermost parts—even the parts we don't know. God knew them before we came into this world. On a scale of one to ten, God's knowledge of us is a perfect ten!

4. This is a more intimate personal-reflection question, and answers will vary among participants.

5. Jesus promises to dine with us. Jesus references a meal, in part, because it's a portrait of a rich relationship where people spend intimate time together.

6. Activities included devotion to the apostles' teaching and fellowship, breaking of bread, prayer, experiencing God's power, spending time together, sharing, giving, meeting together regularly, and eating together in their homes. All of these brought the believers closer together and deepened their relationships.

7, 8. Answers will vary among participants.

✦Digging Deeper✦

Despite Elijah's zeal, the Israelites did not listen. They rejected God's covenant, tore down the altars, and killed the prophets. Elijah complains that he is the only one left and now his life is in danger. Relationships are crucial. God uses other people in our lives to encourage us, strengthen us, correct us, and reflect his love in our lives. Like Elijah, when we are isolated, we are more susceptible to fear, depression, and discouragement.

Chapter 6: Free to Be Yourself

Focus: God has given you a unique blend of gifts, talents, passion, and personality that is designed to be used for his glory. Fear should never limit your ability to honor God with what you have been given.

1. This icebreaker question challenges participants to reflect on their unique blend of gifts, talents, passions, and interests.

2. Bezalel's gifts include the skill, ability, and knowledge to make artistic designs for work in metals including gold, silver, and bronze, the ability to cut and set stones, work in wood, and engage in all kinds of craftsmanship. Oholiab was appointed as a helper. Together, they used their gifts and talents for the building of the tabernacle.

3. Moses called those who were skilled and those who were willing to work. It's possible for someone to be skilled but unwilling to work and vice versa. That's why it's important to not only use and develop your talents but also to keep a willing heart.

4. When one part of the body chooses not to function properly, shut down, or spend its energy trying to be something it's not, the whole body suffers. When every part works as it's designed, the whole body functions well.

5. This is a more intimate personal-reflection question and answers will vary among participants.

6. Fear caused the servant to hide his talent. The other two servants responded differently because they were not bound by fear.

7. Jesus is trying to communicate that it doesn't matter how much you have been given, but what's important is how you use what you've been given.

8. Answers will vary among participants.

✦Digging Deeper✦

As the participants share, look for ways to build camaraderie, support, and encouragement among the women.

Chapter 7: Fear of Lack—God as Provider

Focus: All of us will face a fear of lack sometime in our lives, but at those moments God wants us to turn to him in faith and discover him as our ultimate provider.

1. This icebreaker question challenges participants to reflect on a time when they were in need and discovered God's faithfulness through the experience.

2. In Psalm 23, the shepherd makes me lie down, leads me beside quiet waters, restores my soul, guides me in paths of rightousness, is with me, comforts me, prepares a table before me, anoints my head with oil. The verbs include: makes, leads, restores, guides, comforts, prepares, and anoints. God provides for us in many ways!

3. Answers will vary among participants.

4. In 1 Kings 17:4, Elijah is fed by the ravens. In 1 Kings 17:13–14 Elijah is fed through the miraculous multiplication of the widow's food supplies. The last two questions are subjective, but it could be argued that God told Elijah to go to the widow so that her (and her son's) needs would also be met. Through his act of obedience as well as her obedience and faith, God provided for all of them.

5. While this question is subjective, one could say that both faith and generosity played a role in her gift. Her faith was greater than her fear of lack. The result of her gift was that her sacrifice was memorized for generations to come through its retelling in the Bible.

6, 8. Answers will vary among participants.

✦DIGGING DEEPER✦

Through this passage, Jesus reveals a simple but powerful truth: namely, that where our treasure is our heart will be also. In other words, the things that have the most value in our lives also have our hearts. Jesus wants us to give our hearts to God and to trust him for everything. He wants us to have an eternal perspective on our earthly possessions and invest our energy into things that will last.

✦PONDER AND PRAY✦

Paul encourages us to do three things when faced with anxiety: pray, petition, and offer thanks to God. We are to take our issues to God, ask him for our needs, and thank him for all that he is and all that he is doing.

Chapter 8: Fear of Loss—God as Protector

Focus: All of us will experience moments in life where everything changes and the life we have known is lost, but at that place God meets us. He is our protector.

1. This icebreaker question challenges participants to reflect on a personal time of loss and discovered God's faithfulness and protection through the experience.

2. Answers will vary among participants.

3. Naomi hoped that her widowed daughters-in-law would remarry. As a result of her actions, Ruth chose to stay with her and made a commitment to go wherever she went. Now neither Naomi nor Ruth were alone!

4. Job lost his oxen, donkeys, servants, sheep, camels, sons, and daughters.

5. Job mourned and then he worshiped. He recognized that all things came from the Lord, they were not his own. And in the midst of it all, he did not sin.

6. Paul has gained a deeper knowledge of Jesus Christ.

7. Stripped of temporal things, we are more freely able to cling to that which is eternal.

8. Answers will vary among participants.

✦Digging Deeper✦

Elijah demands that the widow give him her son. As a result, Elijah takes the son, prays, and God restores the boy. When we give our losses to God, we discover him more deeply and fully as our Protector and Provider.

Chapter 9: Fear of Death—God as Redeemer

Focus: As a believer, death has no hold on us or our dreams, and God has promised us not only a purpose but a new home that's beyond our imagination.

1. This icebreaker question challenges participants to reflect on a personal time of disappointment and discovered God's faithfulness through the experience.

2. Answers will vary among participants.

3. • Psalm 48:14—He will be our guide even to the end.

- Psalm 49:15—He will redeem our life and take us to himself.
- Psalm 73:26—God is enough. He is the strength of our heart and portion forever.
- Proverbs 14:32—Even in death the righteous have a refuge.
- John 3:15—Everyone who believes in Jesus will have eternal life.

4. Within the context, Jesus was speaking of his own death, but he was also pointing to a kingdom principle that sometimes something must die in order to come to new life. Answers will vary among participants, but all kinds of plants and trees appear to die in the fall only to come to back to a new life in the spring. As followers of Jesus, we go through the process of dying in order to live the full life God designed for us.

5. Both a seed falling to the earth and pruning involve some kind of death in order to be brought to new life. This is a paradox of sorts, but through it Jesus illustrates that some things must come to an end in order to have a new beginning.

6. Answers will vary among participants.

7. They were able to testify that no matter what happened in the furnace, their faith remained in God. And not only did King Nebuchadnezzar get to see an angel, but as a result of their faith, he issued a decree that no one could speak against the one, true God.

8. Answers will vary among participants.

✦Digging Deeper✦

Because of God's panoramic perspective, God looks at the death of the saints differently than we do. Through death we pass from this world and into the world to come, namely, heaven. This is not a time of mourning. This is a time when every tear is wiped away.

Chapter 10: Embracing His Love

Focus: A healthy understanding of God and the fear of God is essential to having a deep relationship with him.

1. This icebreaker question challenges participants to reflect on how their relationships with their earthly fathers affect their understandings of their heavenly Father.

2. Answers will vary among participants.

3. God asks that we observe God's commands, walk in his ways, and revere him. God asks that we praise him and not forget him, thus thinking that we did it all on our own without him. God promises that he will provide a good land rich with water and food and precious metals. God's provision is richly abundant.

4. God disciplines us out of his love and in order to draw us back into relationship with himself.

5. God disciplines us so that we may share in his holiness. He disciplines us because he is a good father and we are his true children. God's discipline produces a harvest of righteousness and peace.

6. Peter may have expected a rebuke, discipline, or even something worse.

7. Jesus rebuked the disciples for their lack of faith and stubborn refusal to believe. But within moments of the rebuke, he sends them out on the Great Commission to take the good news of Jesus to the ends of the earth. The disciples responded by obeying.

8. Answers will vary among participants.

✦DIGGING DEEPER✦

Peter jumped into the water to get to Jesus faster while the other disciples brought the catch into shore. While Peter exhibited passion for Jesus, the disciples exhibited responsibility for their catch. Both are healthy responses. After eating, Jesus turns to Peter and addresses him directly. He asks Peter about his love and commitment, and then Jesus prophesies over Peter about his future. He tells him of things that will happen to him, but he concludes by reminding Peter that despite the outcome the calling remains the same: Follow me. Despite the denials, Jesus's love for Peter never changed. His calling as a disciple never changed. This is a beautiful portrait of God's all-embracing love.

Chapter 11: Sharing Your Faith

Focus: The truth is that the good news of Jesus Christ is too good to keep to ourselves. We are called to overcome our fears and share our faith with others.

1. This icebreaker question challenges participants to reflect on any fears they have when it comes to sharing their faith.

2. Answers will vary among participants.

3.
- Andrew heard about Jesus from John the Baptist.
- Simon (Peter) heard about Jesus from Andrew.
- Philip heard about Jesus from Jesus.
- Nathaniel heard about Jesus from Philip.

God primarily uses us to spread the good news of Jesus. Introducing someone to Jesus simply means telling someone about him. God is ultimately responsible for their salvation, but we are part of his plan to get the word out!

4. The elements of the Great Commission include: Go and make disciples; baptize them; teach them to obey everything that Jesus commanded.

5–8. Answers will vary among participants

Chapter 12: Trusting God with All the Details

Focus: God wants us to trust all the details and small issues in our lives to him along with the big issues we encounter. Nothing is too big or to small for him to handle.

1. This icebreaker question challenges participants to reflect on moments when they've struggled to give something over to God through prayer.

2. Answers will vary among participants.

3. Mary could have feared the angel's message as well as rejection from Joseph, her family, or the Jewish community.

4. Mary's response is focused on God. He is her source of strength and hope and the focus of her worship. Her response challenges us to turn to God first during uncertain times.

5. Circumstances had to be just as Jesus predicted—with the donkey, colt, and person willing let them go.

6. This detail fulfilled an age-old prophecy concerning the coming of Jesus.

7, 8. Answers will vary among participants.

✦Digging Deeper✦

The disciples responded in fear, while Jesus responded with faith.

✦About the Author✦

Margaret Feinberg is an author and speaker who offers a refreshing perspective on faith and the Bible. She has written more than a dozen books including *The Sacred Echo* and *The Organic God*. Margaret is a popular speaker at women's events, luncheons, and retreats as well as national conferences including Catalyst, LeadNow, Fusion, and the National Pastor's Conference.

She lives in Morrison, Colorado, in the shadow of the Rockies with her 6'8" husband, Leif. When she's not writing and traveling, she loves hiking, shopping, blogging, laughing, and drinking skinny vanilla lattes with her girlfriends. But some of her best days are spent communicating with her readers.

So if you want to put a smile on her face, go ahead and write her!

Margaret@margaretfeinberg.com

www.margaretfeinberg.com

www.margaretfeinberg.blogspot.com

Tag her on Facebook or follow her on twitter

www.twitter.com/mafeinberg

✦ NOTES ✦

✦ Notes ✦

✦ Notes ✦

✦ Notes ✦

✦ Notes ✦

✦ Notes ✦

WOMEN OF FAITH
DEVOTIONAL JOURNAL

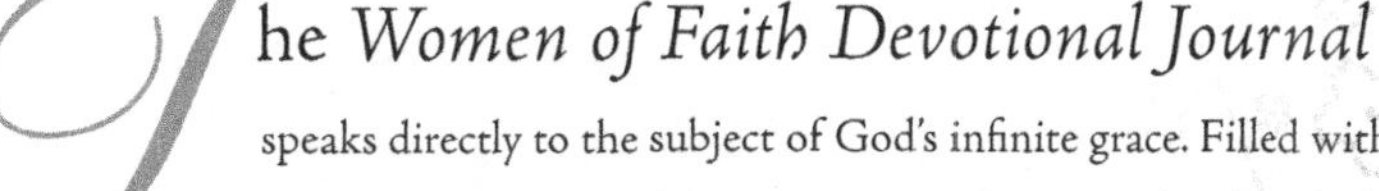

The Women of Faith Devotional Journal speaks directly to the subject of God's infinite grace. Filled with stirring quotes and uplifting Scripture, this journal is the ideal addition to any devotional time.

- Scripture verses highlight wisdom for daily life
- Your favorite Women of Faith speakers' enlightening thoughts on grace
- Plenty of writing space to record dreams, hopes, and personal reflections